DELIRIUM
OF THE
WISE

DELIRIUM OF THE WISE

A Collection of Poetry and Spoken Word

PJ

PHOENIX JAMES

DELIRIUM OF THE WISE

First Edition: 2022

ISBN: 978-1-7397925-6-5 (Paperback)
ISBN: 978-1-7397925-7-2 (Ebook)

Cover Artwork & Design by Phoenix James.
Book Design & Formatting by Phoenix James.

Visit the author's website at www.PhoenixJamesOfficial.com or email him at phoenix@PhoenixJamesOfficial.com

DEDICATION

To all the ones who love
To all the ones who lose
To all who find the message
Amidst the madness
And to all who find joy
In all the sadness
I hope this delights you

And to a young boy
A long time ago
Who looking beyond the surface
Always had questions
And thoughts outside of the box
Who always challenged the norm
And defiantly pushed the boundaries
Look what you've done

Thank you for your fearlessness
And your wild and beautiful mind
They have kept and served me well

I hope this meets your expectations
And you're overwhelmed with pride.

CONTENTS

ADORABLE

I think
I'm going to just
Continue admiring you
From a distance
And no more than that
I think it's best that way
I don't want to get close
Only to find out
That you are not
As beautiful
On the inside
As you are on the outside
That we don't connect
In all the ways
I thought we might
Or that I'm not the knight
In shining armour
That you'd hoped for
You're adorable
I want to keep you that way
And remain your hero.

AWKWARD

Our first meeting
First date
First kiss
First night
Mad
Passionate
Freaky
Hot
Wet
Messy
Sticky
Sweaty
Dirty
Rampant
Wild
Horny sex
Next morning
I love you
You're not going anywhere
You're mine
We're going to have babies
You drive me crazy
I'm marrying you
I don't care

2

We're going to be together
Forever
I think that scared her away
She hasn't called
Since I said it
Any thoughts?

BEAST

They should
Have never ever
Let you out
From wherever it is
You came from
I promise you
I am going to hunt you down
For as long as it takes
Until I capture you
In my claws
Then I'm going to mate with you
Like a wild horny beast
And then
Probably trap you
In my jaws again
And continue eating you
You look too yummy
And delicious
To be roaming around
So freely
In your case
This jungle
Is strictly
For lovemaking.

4

BEAUTIFUL

You have
The most
Beautiful face
No seriously
I just get lost
In your eyes
It's like
Watching a movie
With the volume
Turned down
Just engaged
In your motion
Your expression
I just love
Looking at you
I'm probably
Sounding crazy right now
But I don't care
I think
You're the most
Beautiful thing
I've ever seen
Truly
You are

I don't even want
To touch you right now
I just want to lay
Here
And look at you.

BEDRIDDEN

If I had my way
You wouldn't go today
Forget getting paid
I'd call up your boss lady
And tell her I've got her slave
Tied up in my bedroom
In three different ways
G-string wrapped around my wrist
Thighs wrapped around my face
I'd tell her you're not in the best state
It's quite a serious case
You'll be away for a few days
And that you'll have to stay in bed
With your ankle bracelet
Jingling above my head.

BITCH

I want to meet the person
Who tells guys
That it looks cool
Fashionable
Or sexy
To wear their jeans
Dropping off
Well below their waste
With their underwear
And ass showing
Because I feel
That maybe
They can educate me further
Because as far as I've been told
That's how the "male bitches"
In prison
Who constantly get fucked
By the other inmates
Have to wear their trousers
Not cool
Not sexy.

BLACKS

It is widely accepted
That Jesus was black
Though some dispute it
Despite all the facts
But he had to be black
Because only blacks
Are ever expected
To suffer like that.

BOASTY

I really hate to say this
But honesty is safest
Your sex
Is not the greatest
Your sex
Is overrated
If your sex is God
Call me an atheist
Sex with you
Equals time wasted
A journey
To all the wrong places
But I do agree
Your sex
Is not to be played with
I'd be safer
Playing in lion cages
Plus
You don't
Look that good naked
And if I was a DJ
Your sex
Would not make the playlist
So stop boasting
Save it.

BONDED

I don't care
How many babies she's got
She could have three more
And I'd still think she's hot
Married or not
We share a bond
That not even time could stop
She's a part of me
And I'm a part of her
We share a frequency
That lives beyond words
Beyond worlds
She calls me Starseed
And she's my Orisha girl
I don't know
What else to tell you
Other than that
Our sex
Is an out of body experience
And that's the facts.

BOUGHT

Yeah
True
Your new man
Might be quite cool
So much for the guy
That really liked you
Since high school
I feel a right fool
So sad to see
That a guy can buy you
Or even try to
Bet he won't
Eat your pussy like I do
I heard
He's a not too bright dude
Who lies to you
Beats
And makes you cry too
Hope you get run over
By his Porsche
And he dies too.

BURNS

I read
That a strong
Male model
Was needed
For the red carpet
So I applied
I was successful
But after
I 'd finished the job
I was totally exhausted
It's the first time
I've ever got carpet burns
From just carrying one.

CHAMPION

I've made the sky
Change colour
Against its will
With a single stare
I've tap danced
On the face of the moon
Without feet
I've held back
The raging seas
With just a fingertip
I've touched the burning sun
With my nose
I've taught little children
How to fly
I've done all this
And many more things
That it is said
No man can do
I've done them all
And will do
So many more
As long as I have you.

CLOSER

I care not
That the earth
Is becoming smaller
That the seas
Are rising
To drown
And consume the planet
That global warming
Is melting the ice caps
That the oceans
Are corroding the coastlines
I threw away
My old atlas
I don't care how much
The new one has changed
The smaller
Our vulnerable
Little island becomes
The better it is
For I pray
That it will close our distance
And drift you
Closer to me
One day.

CLOWNS

Perhaps we're all
Just dancing monkeys
Summoned
To entertain the crowds
Buskers
Tap dancing for peanuts
Maybe we're all just clowns
No-one ever noticing
Our tears
Or that our smiles
Are upside down
Too busy
Seeking dreams
That like ours
Will never be found
Maybe we're the court jesters
Who end up
Wearing the custard pies
Maybe the joke is on us
Like donkeys
With carrots
Dangling before our eyes.

COME

She laid down
Next to me
Smelling sweet
Like confectionary
Caressing me sexually
She used her tongue
Not just specially
But exceptionally
She challenged me
Intellectually
When she read my mind
Like telepathy
And said
I know you want sex with me
I said
Yes, definitely
She said
Well, come and get me
But wear Durex please
And don't make a mess in me
I'm not looking for a pregnancy
Or an STD.

CONVERSATION

Politics
God
Jesus
And religion
Spirituality
Drugs in the community
And the criminal justice system
Bush and Obama
Having blood ties
Or even 1997
The year Osama Bin Laden died
Could speak on gun possession
And knife crime
Underage pregnancies
And teenage suicides
Deaths in police custody
The war on Iraq
And reparations
The recession
Secret societies
Better schooling
And education
Oops! Sorry
Wrong conversation.

COSY

Locked out of home
Garage door
Finally closed properly
Keeping the world out
Electric heater
Full of dust
But works
Feels like
A hot summer in Antigua
I think this is
The most cosiest
And relaxed
I've ever felt
Anywhere
Blankets
From the boot
Of your dads old car
Which we've hardly used
A cassette
Filled with old soul classics
Marvin
Sings to us live
This is the best place
On earth
To be right now.

CREAM

I met a hot little thing on the scene
Performs fellatio like it's her dream
We haven't even spoke
Yet she deep-throats like a machine
It's no joke
Yes, I know it's obscene
But I can't cope
If you know what I mean
I had to cut some rope
And tie her up like a goat
So I could taste her ice cream
And it was nice cream
And I like cream
So I licked and licked
Until she gave a high scream
Like I screamed.

DANCE

Let's dance
Like we created feet
And manufactured the shoes
Dancing to our own beat
Like no one else can do
Let's not just dance
Like we own the floor
But more like
The world is our stage
And it's us they came out for
Let's dance
Like no-one is looking
When we know that they are
Let's dance
Like the main attraction
Let's dance like superstars
Let us dance
With a passion
And make the magic happen.

DARKNESS

I'm crouched down
In the pitch black darkness
Holding my bow and arrow
And staring the devil
Right in his face
Yes
Right now
He's totally shocked
He can't believe
How perfect my eyesight is
And how perfectly accurate
My aim is
He's bleeding
I'm preparing my arrow again
And thinking to myself
He ain't seen nothing yet.

DINNER

Turn up here
For dinner
Gift wrapped
In your sexiest thong
With some sexy high heels
And your ankle bracelet on
Don't worry about clothes
You won't have them on for long
Just wear a coat
And whatever else you want
Leave your phone at home
There won't be
Any opportunities to speak
In fact
You'll be speechless
When you see how well I eat
And I don't mean the food
So hurry it up, sweetness
I'm talking about you.

DREAMS

Long before
I'd ever heard the words
Time makes dreams defer
I had defaced every clock face
And replaced them
With images of her
So now I only picture
The face
Of a missed universe
She gives my dreams
Their place
And worth
While mother nature
Remains
Lost for words
Clutching
At the fading skirt
Of mother earth
I'm disco dancing
With eternity
She vows to serve me
Time fades
It's cursed
I dream
Eternally.

ENERGY

The universe is energy
We are part of that energy
It is constant
It's both within us
And around us
We are affected by it
We all feel the same things
At different times
Often at the same time too
Depending on where
We each are mentally
Physically
And spiritually
At that time
How we respond to it
We are free to determine
Every aspect of it
Is servant
Or master
Success
Or failure
To he who chooses.

EXES

It's expected
That your exes
Will have sex with
Whoever they get with
After they get rid
Of who they messed with
Before they stepped with
Who they've now met with
So don't be vexed with
Or upset with
Your exes
Because their sex is
Now someone else's
Don't forget this
Just respect this
And you too
Will find and get with
Your next fix
Do you get this?

FEELINGS

I could have you
In a minute
I know it
And you know it too
But the thing is
You also know
That you'd never have me
As your "man"
And really I wouldn't
Waste your time
Just for sex
It's not my style
I rather connect
With women who
Feel the same as me
And we know
What it's about
And we aim
Not to catch feelings
In the process
But we're both human
And sometimes
It's inevitable
And unavoidable
But we aim not to.

FERAL

Well
If that's your wife
She wasn't that night
Flirting all up in the club
With her skirt real tight
Dancing to Beyoncé
Like she'd had too many drinks
Ask any female
About the drunk girl
With her face in the sink
At the end of the night
After she'd left the club twice
And then for a third time
With a guy on a motorbike
If that's your lady
I don't know what to say
If that's her
She wasn't that day.

FOREVER

I am not Icarus
These wings
Do not melt
I don't fall
From the sky
I resurrect
The self
I die
And live
Eternal life
In forever
I shall dwell
Amen.

FRIENDS

Waiting
And relying on
The support of friends
Is very often
Like standing
By your cooker
And relying
On the fish
To jump
From the river
Straight into
Your frying pan.

FYI

For your information
Lest it be
In varying degrees
Dismissed
And overlooked

Though it is
Not as openly
And freely stated
As once upon a time
Not so long ago gone by

Many places
Across the globe
Are still not hiring
Negroes.

GATHER

If
My eyes
Should see
The eternal shade
Before I finish
All I have to say
May you each
Add one of my writings
To a page
And read it aloud
Beside my grave
To all and any
Who gather in my name
May you also exchange
Words of your own
About the reasons
Why you came
Bring photos
And notes
Share our jokes
And pains
Recall
One of my quotes
Then recite it

Along with a poem
You wrote
Pause a while
And then smile.

GIFT

He creates
Like he's got a disease
But he is not
Dis-eased by it
He is more
Eased by it
Relieved by it
Pleased by it
He is past the days
Of please buy it
Please try it
He loses either way
Regardless
Of how high he prices it
It's priceless
And he realises it
So all that matters now
Is if he likes it
And it's both his gift
And his curse
But what would be worse
Is if he himself
Never realised
Its worth.

GLOOM

I'm as drunk
As a skunk
Or an alcoholic monk
On a Sunday afternoon
What happens next
Is anyone's guess
But the answers
Better come soon
I'm drowning my sorrows
Not worrying about tomorrow
I'm amused
Like it's all a cartoon
And maybe it is
Maybe I'm too serious
Or maybe I'm just
Headed for doom
Perhaps I believe too much
Perhaps not enough
Perhaps being delusional
Keeps me
Over the moon.

GO

Seconds turn into minutes
Minutes turn into hours
Hours turn into days
Days turn into weeks
Weeks turn into months
Months turn into years
And your best days
Will have passed you by
Like a thief in the night
While you were fast asleep
In your bed
Or flutter away
Like a butterfly
While you were daydreaming
At your desk
Don't waste another second
Of the time
That you have left.

GOALS

I often end up
Going well beyond
The initial mark I aimed for
In achieving my goals
It's not something
I do intentionally
It just happens automatically
Like a mechanism
Like neurolinguistic programming
Pavlov's dogs
Or any reticular activating system
I've learned
It can be both a positive
And negative thing
I guess overall
It's about flexibility
Keeping the initial aim
In view
And knowing when to stop.

GONE

Wow
You were beautiful
Captured you for a moment
Don't know
What I was thinking
I let you go
Perhaps too consumed
In pursuing dreams
Perhaps we both were
Distracted
Maybe I should've
Made you
More a part of mine
Maybe you were
But I didn't know
Or even realise
Couldn't see
Blinded by ambition
Perhaps
Either way
You're not here now
Because like a fool
I didn't dream
That my net
Might have a hole in it.

HEAVEN

If they should
Turn us away
From the gates of heaven
For our sins
And indiscretions
We will sit down
Together
Outside
Observing
The good ones
Pass by
And we will eat
Drink
Laugh
And be merry
And share
Precious stories
About the best times
Of our lives.

HEROES

I salute you
My courageous
And heroic sister
Say it loud
And proud
Because the lifting
Of one voice
Is liberation
For the crowd
No matter how awkward
Or profound
Or how crazy it sounds
As long as you continue
To express
You'll always wear
That 'S' on your chest
Too many now
Are afraid to say
What they really feel
Wow
I guess in speaking out
It makes us all heroes for real
Much more
Increased
Power to you.

ICON

I hope to be
Remembered
And regarded
As both
A great creator
And a good person
So somewhere
Between
God and Jesus.

INSPIRED

Ladies
And Gentlemen
It is completely
Without regret
That I inform you
That as wonderful
Eccentric
Flamboyant
Exotic
And fabulous
As I am
I would be
Totally remiss
If I didn't take it upon myself
At this time
And see it
As my royal
And honourable duty
To express
To you
Just how much
I am humbled
Excited
Uplifted

And inspired
To witness others
In relentless pursuit
Of goals
And dreams too
I honour your passion.

INTRODUCTION

He says
He needs no introduction
But he's written
A whole essay
I had to laugh at that
I don't know about you guys
But I fell asleep
Spelling mistakes
Appeared beyond redemption too
He can't possibly be serious
Personally
I think
He's really actually a comedian
Instead
Posing as
Whatever he is claiming to be
And he's good at it
He definitely made me laugh my ass off
After all that talk
He better deliver.

KILLERS

Has anyone heard
Any more
About the young couple
Last year
Who both contracted HIV
And were going around separately
Meeting people online for dates
Having sex
And infecting people
On purpose
That's like serial killers
Or couples who kill
On a whole different level
Are they white
Are they black
I guess
Obviously
Their victims
Aren't too keen
On coming forward
With info
To help identify them
They should
Be safe.

KNOW

If our minds
Are always thinking
And developing
And new thoughts
Are continually being formed
While our bodies
Are also constantly growing
And going through changes
And we cannot
At anytime
Determine each
And every action
We are yet to take
When does the time come
When we can truly say
We know ourselves
Or others.

LEGEND

Your life
Was much like mine
Except
I notice now
Your eyes
Ceased to shine
They lost their gleam
They no longer dreamed
They died
I pray for wisdom
But never to see
The side you've seen
In your lifetime
And it must be worse
Than death
Even I would sacrifice
My breath
In the next
Just to be sure
I wouldn't have to walk
The path you've left
Nevertheless
You are still here
In me
And we
Are legend.

LIFESAVER

Naturally
I was attracted to you
At first sight
As I was drawn closer
You moved further away
I never understood it
Until this very morning
In my shyness
And hesitance
At that time
And the distance
You seemingly created
We consciously
Subconsciously
And unconsciously
Died prematurely
Upon reading your confession
I realise now
That this dying
Was not without necessity
You saved our lives
And I thank you.

MEMORIES

Yeah
Me too
We need to get together
It's been a while
Feels like forever
Since I've seen that smile
Or laughed with you
Doing things
We used to do
Like watching movies
And eating junk food
In the early hours
Playing our music
And sharing showers
Dancing like lunatics
The world was ours
Joking and play acting
Like we were on stage
The love making
And the passion
I miss those days.

MENTAL

I'm a reckless recluse
Drunk off of you
With a quill
And inkwell
Stuck to the inside
Of my forehead
With super glue
And only those
Who think like me
Will understand
The methods
To the madness
That I do
Or say
But who cares anyway
I'm drowning in lunatics
Who couldn't tell you
The time of day
Even if it flashed
Its most important life lessons
Right in front of their face
So what do I think?
Pour me another drink.

MOMENTS

We awaken
I'm still tipsy
From last night
It's early
You look at me
Looking at you
Through morning eyes
We smile
You kiss my lips
Softly
Then sail away
Into sleep again
On my chest
The radio plays
Old mellow love songs
I think how much
I've missed your familiar smell
I just want to hold you
Closer than ever before
I close my eyes
And feel your breathing
This will be
The most beautiful
Moment of my day.

MORNING

I was walking
Down the road
On my way to a photoshoot
And crossed paths
With a lady
In a lovely black dress
Coming out of the cemetery
As I went by
I politely said
Morning
She replied
*Hi, yes I am. It's my dad, I just left his
funeral*
I said
Oh sorry, I meant good morning
She said
How can it be a good morning
You fucking idiot
I just told you my dad died.

MOUTH

It's not hot sex
If he won't go south
He's got a lot of talk
But can't use his mouth

I'm not supporting these boys
Who say that it's nasty
But want their dicks sucked
That bit gets past me
Plus you say
He always comes before you do
Now to me
That can't be fun
You need to trade him in
And get yourself another one

Because it's not hot sex
If he won't go south
He's got a lot of talk
But can't use his mouth.

MOUTH II

As I keep saying, love
It's not hot sex
If he won't go south
He's got a lot of talk
But can't use his mouth

Just wants to hold out his dick
For you to go down and lick
But loses his tongue
When it comes to the real fun
If you ask me, hun
I don't support that one
So as I said before
And I'm going to say it once more

It's not hot sex
If he won't go south
He's got a lot of talk
But can't use his mouth.

MOVES

Excited
And I haven't even started yet
Show me those moves again
Lest I forget
How to disco dance with death
How to advance my steps
And enhance my breath
Until I need not rest
How to take fire from my chest
And transfer it to my legs
How to land on my head
And still shake hands with the best
How to physically express
Far more than any would expect
How to move off beat
But still keep it all in context
Yes.

NEXT

I find it needless
To highlight
That the greater percentage
Of women
Want to find a "good man"
However
I feel I would be remiss
If I wrote on this subject
In any capacity
And failed to express
A view
In addition
That an almost
Equally great percentage
Of those women
Usually have no idea
What to do
With that "good man"
Once they find him
In relation
To basic understanding
Self conduct
Interaction
And communication.

NOW

I may receive
A bunch of flowers
If I'm sick
Perhaps a few more
After I die
But I won't need
Any flowers then
I want them
When I'm healthy
And alive.

PAUSE

My friends
Because I love you like brothers
I will share this for free
The next time
You and her
Find yourselves
Arguing in the street
With your voices raising
And you feel yourselves
Getting heated
I want you
To suddenly just stop
Stop thinking
About your response
Stop moving
Stop talking
Pause everything
Then
I want you to just
Grab her
And hug her
Firmly
With both arms
And just
Stay there
Regardless.

PEACEMAKER

He had to stop
And go back
To roll up his sleeves
And get down
On his knees
And dig
Very deep down
Into his past
Before he could find
And summon
The strength within
To dust himself off
And stand tall
And look forward
Boldly into his future
He says it was worth it
He got a little dirty
And a few scratches
And scrapes
That he says will heal
Only to make him stronger
For the journey ahead
He says
He recommends it
Highly.

PLANS

House
And land
My friends
House and land
Too many
Build their houses
On quicksand
Cement your plans
Or see them demolished
By the quicksilver man
Those who are quick
To recognise metaphor
Will understand.

PLEASED

Tell them
It's not your fault
That you can't stop
Talking about the sex
Tell them
If they had it
Nearly as good as you
Then they wouldn't get upset
Tell them
Don't be mad at you
Because their man
Fails to impress
While yours never fails
To keep your panties wet
Tell them
Don't be vexed
Because your man
Eats you
Until it makes a mess
Weakens your legs
And makes you cum so hard
It leaves you gasping for breath
Tell them.

POSSIBLE

If I'm honest with you
I feel like
Anything is possible
I base that belief
On things I have learned
And experienced
As well as
My own achievements thus far
They are not the world
But they are a part of mine
Part of what is possible
As humble as they may be
I am content
In knowing
That I've done more
Than I ever hoped
Or thought I could do
I aim higher still
I am blessed to inspire
Whilst also discovering me.

PRAYING

I'm a dirty drunken swine
Salsa dancing naked
With the devil
Outside your church door
On Christmas eve
Blaspheming
And shouting profanities
Up at the stained glass window
With the cross
And christ-like figure on it
Tongue kissing
A prostitute
Smoking marijuana
Rolled in scriptures
From the book of revelations
And
Miraculously
I'm still
More godly than you
Will ever be
I'll pray for you.

PREPARE

My heart hurts
For you, brother
Having children
Doesn't necessarily mean
You'll be together
Forever
I too like you
Once believed it was so
Or should be
A year on
She's telling you
She would rather be single
She says
The confines
Of the relationship
Suffocate her
I wish
Someone
Could have prepared you
I wish
They could have prepared me
I wish
They could have prepared us
I hope
Someone will prepare others
I love you.

PRICELESS

Growing up
My whole life
And even to this very day
I've heard that sex sells
But unfortunately for me
I've never been able
To price mine accordingly
To its true worth
Or find a big enough box
Or strong enough carrier bag
Suitable wrapping paper
Fancy enough packaging
Or worthy enough delivery driver
I think
I'm just going to have to
Sell it naked
With a tag attached
That reads
Priceless.

PURSUE

The word Pursuit
Looks like Pur-su-it
Which sounds like Pursue it
And if your heart is in it
Then I think you should do it.

QUESTION

If you only had
A certain amount
Of time
Left in life
To fulfil
All your goals
Ambitions
Dreams
And desires
What would you do?
I don't want to know
Your answer
I just wanted
To remind you
In case you were busy
Wasting precious time
If your time
Should be up
Too soon
And you
Suddenly realise
You haven't achieved
Even half
Of the things you said

You would do
I don't want you
To blame me
I'm your friend.

RAPTURE

We've been down here
For two hours
Enjoying
The acoustic performers
Listening intently
It's beautiful
Another hour passes
A soul singer
From Chicago
Isn't singing
He's spinning records
In a basement
Filled with tourists
His devout followers
In the heart of London
Dancing
Like it's the last time
They'll ever hear music
Drinking like fish
We too get caught up
In the rapture
We rise
And become believers.

REMEMBERED

I am one of those
Types of people
Who hopes
That when I finally
Leave this world
For good
That I will be
Remembered
As someone
Who gave back to it
Much more than I took.

RESCUED

I survived
The Amazon Jungle
Where I once suffered
Pain and torture
Was rescued
By a beautiful Brazilian
And then escaped
To Hollywood
Where I found promise
Of a better tomorrow.

RESERVED

I suggest a new law
Where the act
Of sexual intercourse
Is strictly only reserved
For those who perform it well
I believe this
To be one of the solutions
To many of life's root conflicts
That arise between people
A persons good sex nature
Should not be tainted
By the bad sex of another
No good can come of it
The necessity is clear
The objective is set
Good sex all the way
Ban bad sex
A better world for all.

RUN

Stay away, son
They'll only hurt you
And hurt you
Until you are painless
And numb
And can't feel anything
For anyone
They'll try to possess you
And if they do
They'll take
And take
And try to change you
Lie to you
And deceive you
Until all you see
Is lies and deceit
Everywhere you go
They'll steal your ability
To trust
To recognise the truth
They'll break you, son
And I can't fix you when they do.

SELFISH

The attractiveness
Of joining male friends
To engage in rampant sex
With a female
Who is more than willing
To share herself with us
And eagerly participate
Has somehow
Lost its appeal
Over the years
I guess I'm more
Of the selfish type
In regards
To the sharing aspect
I believe it's safe to say
I will always
Be more into one-to-one
Sexual engagements
This isn't to say
It wasn't great
Have fun
Be safe.

SHUFFLE

Look
We started
This dance together
And we shall end
This dance together
So never mind too much
My occasional outbursts
That would cause you to question
My ability
To keep up this shuffle
Because if you look
At my feet
When I'm cursing
You will notice
Even then
That they never stop moving
Often
I just feel the need
To add some spice
Remember
When your feet
Were getting tired
Someone
Had to
Continue the show.

SLAVE

She's triple X rated
I just can't take it
She's always naked
Her bedroom
Is like the making
Of a blue movie
Called play thing
And I'm her slave thing
Hers for the taking
This constant raping
From Miss wanton
And craving
She's a strange thing
She just says things
And I swear
My underwear
Vanishes
Into thin air
She's amazing
And I'm not complaining
I'm just stating
I wouldn't change a thing
No hating.

SMART

The familiar
"Work smart
Not hard"
Only works
Depending
On how smart
You are.

SWEETS

Honey
He's probably just bored
Men get bored
Women too
We all just
Get bored sometimes
Or just want to
Have our cake and eat it
Have sex
With different people
Like enjoying different foods
At a buffet
Or variety of sweets
In a sweet shop
Or like sampling cocktails
I don't know
If I am excusing him
For the sake of myself
But I do know
It's a natural desire
It's just about those
Willing to control
And suppress it.

TODAY

My friend
Honestly
If you did quit it all today
I wouldn't blame you
If you threw in the towel
Handed in your chips
And just walked away
Today
I wouldn't have anything to say
If you threw off your gloves
And said you'd had enough
I'd just say okay
If you threw down your guns
To the floor
And put your hands in the air
That's fair
Because today
I feel I don't have the right
To tell you
To hang in there.

TRICKS

I am
As I always was
And always will be
The gods saw it fit
So why should I change me
Now it doesn't quite sit
You're quick to blame me
Quick to flip
But you no longer faze me
With games and tricks
Which seek to shame me
I am not Roger Rabbit
You can't frame me
You'll never gain profit
From trying to maim me
You made your bed
But you never made me
Your heart
Is as black as night
And that's all they can see.

TWO-FACED

That man of yours
Fazing you
With meaningless phrases
And thoughts
Serenading you
With his crazy talk
None of which
He really supports
Taking you for walks
Rides
And goose chases
Your man
With two sides
Two faces
But that's the man you chose
So I guess you take it
It's obvious
You're not happy
Or you wouldn't be here
Naked
And though you know
You shouldn't be here
We also know
You shouldn't be there
Face it.

UNPROTECTED

Mister
She just met you
At the club
Eight weeks ago
You both left together
And had unprotected sex
That same night
You've both agreed
You're not looking
For a serious relationship
And just having fun
You've been having
Unprotected sex
Together
Ever since that night
What makes you believe
She's only having
Unprotected sex
With you
Same question
To you too
Little Miss.

WANT

A man
Wanting to be with a woman
And wanting to be with her sexually
Are often
Two very different things
It is in her interest
To find out exactly which
Of the two it is
Perhaps it's both
But she should avoid herself
Any wasted time
Unnecessary misunderstandings
And confusion later on
If he is a real man
He will tell her the truth
If she is woman enough
She will appreciate his honesty
Same goes for men.

WELCOME

I don't care
If you're black
White
Red
Blue
Yellow
With purple spots
Male
Female
Or in-between
Religious
Non religious
Spiritualist
Atheist
Agnostic
Rich
Poor
Married
Single
Or in-between
Heterosexual
Gay
Lesbian
Bi-sexual

Meat eater
Vegetarian
Or in-between
Wide
Long
Short
Tall
Skinny
Or fat
I am Phoenix James
I am your friend
And that's that
No in-between.

WHORE

Smiling
She took me
To a dimly lit room
Where I could smell
The sweet scent of perfume
And as she lay herself
Diagonally across the bed
She looked at me
And said
Take me
I'm yours
I know
This
Is what
You've been waiting for
And I want you too
So come in
And close the door
But before we do
I want us to explore
I want you to taste me
Until I can take no more
Then I want you take me
And make me your whore.

WISDOM

I consider it wise
To surround yourself
With good talkers
Who walk well
The walk
That they talk
That's good
But to surround yourself
With only bad talkers
Who do not walk
The walk
That they talk
Is just plain foolishness.

WISHLIST

Wow
You're very sexy
Incredibly
Thank you
For the birthday message
You sent me
Now I know
What to tell others
To get me
You
Gift wrapped
Specially
And sent to me
Sent to pleasure me
Endlessly
I love your energy
And since you're single
Presently
You're perfect
It's meant to be
Can't wait to open you
Eventually
Oh how much fun
Plenty

I don't know
Where you came from
But we're now
More than friends
To me.

ABOUT THE AUTHOR

Phoenix James is an award winning Writer, Poet, Author and Spoken Word Recording Artist. He began performing his poetic words live on stages across the UK in 1998. His debut spoken word poetry album, *The A.R.T.I.S.T,* was released in 2000. His first limited edition printed collection of poetry, *To Whom It May Concern,* was published in 2003. He has toured and performed his poetry internationally since 2004. He has appeared in films, on television and radio shows, and collaborated with other artists, singer-songwriters, actors, musicians, filmmakers and producers. In 2013, he wrote, directed and produced the feature length mock documentary film, *Love Freely but Pay for Sex.* Phoenix James has written, recorded and released several spoken word poetry albums including, *Phenzwaan Now & Forever* (2009), *A Patchwork Remedy for A Broken Melody* (2020), *FREE* (2021), *Haven for the Tormented* (2021), *With All That Said* (2022), and *Remixes* Volumes: 1 & 2 (2022).

If you enjoyed reading this book, please leave a review online. The author reads every review and they help new readers discover his work.

PHOENIX JAMES

Photo by Phoenix James

Phoenix James lives in London, England.

Connect with Phoenix James on his online social media platforms via www.linktr.ee/ Phoenix_James and say you've read this book. To contact or learn more about Phoenix James and his creative journey or to receive updates via his Newsletter Mailing List, visit his official website at www.PhoenixJamesOfficial.com

Phoenix James Official